# Facing The People

# Facing The People

# Facing The People

*by*

*Martin D'Arcy, S.J.*

DIMENSION BOOKS

Wilkes-Barre, Pennsylvania

First American Edition Edition 1968
by Dimension Books, Inc.

*Nihil Obstat:* Rt. Rev. Msgr. James T. Clark
Censor Librorum
October 16, 1967

*Imprimatur:* ✠ J. Carroll McCormick
Bishop of Scranton
October 18, 1967

Library of Congress Catalog Number 68-13730

# TABLE OF CONTENTS

PAGE

Facing The People .................. 1

Tunic without Seam................. 15

On Laughter ...................... 19

Development of Doctrine........... 23

The Coming of Christ.............. 27

God and Evil...................... 31

Joy in Knowledge ................. 35

Flesh and Spirit................... 39

Our Unchanging God.............. 41

On Freedom...................... 43

The New Name ................... 45

Good Sense in Religion............ 47

The Cross Is Our Hope ............ 51

On Obedience ................... 58

Still Small Voice ................... 62

On Holiness ...................... 65

Answers to Prayer................. 69

The Supernatural ................. 73

# TABLE OF CONTENTS

PAGE

The Good News of Easter............ 77

On Snobbery ...................... 79

Our Abiding City ................. 81

A Luminous Mystery ............... 83

Exiles from Home.................. 87

Open-Eyed ....................... 89

Closed-Eyes ..................... 91

A Reasonable Obedience ........... 93

Knowing God..................... 97

Man's Strength and Weakness ........101

The Plan of Redemption............104

The Christ of The Apostles..........105

He Descended into Hell.............109

Providence and Equilibrium.........113

On Suffering ....................117

Conscience ......................121

The Messianic Hope...............127

# I

# Facing The People

It was not so long ago that Catholic enthusiasts for the Mass complained that its sacrificial nature had been obscured by excessive devotion to the Blessed Sacrament and to the Real Presence. At once, the progressives demanded altars which really looked like altars. Tabernacles and adornments should be conspicuous by their absence. A fresh opportunity was given to artists in the shaping of these bare, simple altars.

But hardly had this movement time to succeed when antiquarians joined with new "progressives" in pronouncing in favor of a table instead of an altar. They claimed that the earliest evidence describes a meal, a eucharistic supper at which many would be gathered together to partake of the consecrated bread and wine and so participate in the mystery of union with Christ.

This latter movements seems for the moment to find most favor. The altar is now more like a table; the priest now faces the people, the language is the vernacular in which all can join, and the ideal is that the altar should be in the center of the church where all can gather 'round the celebrant.

These variations are natural or at any rate intelligible, because the Mass is a unique action with multiple features. It is both a divine action and a human one; a very personal commitment to God and a communal one; it contains both thanksgiving and self oblation and it is a sacrament of union — a sacrifice so rich in mystery that it is no wonder different ages seize upon one feature to the comparative neglect of others. Leon Bloy called it "a holocaust to the accompaniment of nuptial songs."

It can appeal to those who weep and to those who rejoice. The Victim of the Mass is the Risen Christ but His passion is never absent. Hence, in the decline of the middle ages, when plagues and wars had brought in their train sorrow, pain and near-despair, it was the Crucifix, the Christ of the Passion, which appealed to worshippers. This devotion may well have obscured for a time the truth that the Eucharistic Victim is the Lord risen from the dead, "the Lamb slain but alive," the source of our faith and hope and charity and the sure token of a glorious life to come.

This mystery of Christ reigning from the cross does not rule out the thought of a Pascal that Christ "will be in agony until the end of time" — suffering in his members who fill up what is wanting in the sufferings of Christ. We recall in the liturgy the love which reconciled us to the Father by dying. Hence, the memory of the first bloody sacrifice is consonant with the offering of an unbloody one, especially as we the members of Christ, who offer in his name, are only too aware of our sin.

At the beginning of Mass, we contritely and dramatically offer our gifts of bread and wine, and call upon the saints to assist us. It is to the Father we speak — Almighty God, and our being together is not yet in the forefront of our minds or prayers. Only when the sound of Christ's coming is heard in the Preface and in the first words of the Canon are the hearts of the faithful lifted up and hope draws near. The tributary is now to be joined to the great River that flows into the ocean of God. Once this happens, once the sacred words of the Consecration have been pronounced, the worshippers realize that they are no longer by themselves, no longer creatures or servants, but members of the very risen body of Christ. The hope changes to a joyous certainty, so sure indeed that in the climax of the Mass — a moment more stratling than that of the Transfiguration on the holy mountain — the triumphant words of praise and adoration are addressed to God through his Beloved Son, Christ — J *through Him, with Him and in Him.* God is now truly in a new sense our Father, *Abba Father.* All now is changed. Peace and Agapé are ours, and we are partakers at the table of the Lord.

It is interesting that until the moment of transubstantiation the prayer of the Church is to God the Father as our Sovereign Lord. We offer sacrifice to Him, bringing token of our complete submission to Him and thus our sacrifice is lifted into one unique sacrifice with the Father's beloved Son. This is what makes the Mass a thanksgiving and a communion as well as an oblation. These constituents are indissolubly linked together. At the present time it would seem as if the devotion of the Church were drawn towards the Mass' significance as a meal, where the members of Christ are united into Christ and into one another. For this reason, the altar is prepared as a communion table, the priest faces the people and con-celebration is permitted on occasions. The congregation sits as it were 'round a table with the priest. The Mass is a family affair, the family of God is emphasized.

All this brings out the nature of what is rightly called the Eucharist. That is true, but other features should not be neglected for we may suffer some loss in our appreciation of the deep mystery in all divine worship. Religion from the beginning has manifested man's feeling for the numinous. "The beginning of wisdom is the fear of the Lord" — a fear that is a sense of awe and indigence in the presence of the divine. No one can see God and live. Moses is blinded, the people fall prostrate, all is hushed when God comes near and speaks. "Be still and know that I am God."

In the higher religions this note of awe is noticeably present — even the original meaning of the word "mystery" conveys the need of silence. Silence and darkness were felt to be appropriate at the sacred moment in the

Eleusinian mystery and ritual and in the worship of Isis and Mithra. In the early Church, this aspect of mystery was prominent and the rubrics of the liturgy safeguarded it. The priest and people all faced the East where the Christ, risen like the dawn, would appear. The early churches, as recent excavation has shown, were so shaped that the altar was in the eastern apse and the priest looking toward the east spoke to God in the name of the people behind him. The language used was not common but hieratic. And when God made himself really present, all bowed and all voices and music were hushed. The desire to have even the words of Consecration spoken aloud and in the vernacular is not in keeping with the sense of awe and man's deep-felt humble relationship to God. Maybe, too, in the past it was felt that a priest with his back to the East and his face expressing very human traits might interfere with the pure adoration of the living God. Be that as it may, the Church has decided to permit and even encourage experiments with an easier and more popular mode of worship. Its desire is to bring the members of the Church into a more living union with Christ and fellowship with one another.

## II

# Tunic without Seam

St. Paul said that "if Christ be not risen, then is our faith vain." By the truth of the risen Christ Christianity stands or falls, and the same is true, I believe, of the message of Christ. If that message suffer change; if it be no longer exactly what the Son of God taught as "the way and the truth and the life," then Christianity has become a man-made religion and has failed. It may be high in aspiration and noble in principle, but it is not the Word of God: it has failed. This is surely the mind of St. Paul who anathematized any who would dare to change his divinely derived teaching.

We have to go further, and say that if there has been any tampering with the message; if, that is, nowhere now in the year 1968 can the identical truth which was preached in 1568, in 1068, in 368 and by the Apostles be heard, then the claim that Christ was really God, who gave us God's own good news of eternal life, must be given up. This may seem a hard saying and ignored by many who call themselves Christians but do not hesitate to modify the gospel teaching and emend the moral and spiritual principles. They are even prepared to condemn centuries of Christianity as wholly darkened by superstition and false doctrines. Like bees which sting, they die themselves.

The reason for this is simple and sad. It is this. If Christ be truly the Son of God and the Word expressing the loving intentions of the Father towards man, then that teaching is distinct from all human moral or spiritual systems. It is the life-giving message intended by God not for one race or for one generation but for all mankind. It is the key to the restoration, reconciliation and exaltation of man. This is what the Apostles thought, what St. Peter meant when he wrote: "You are called out of darkness into his marvellous light . . . All flesh is grass . . . but the word of God endures for ever. Now this is the word of the gospel which was preached to you." This is the new covenant of God with man. But if within one generation or after many generations the terms of it are glossed, or grow uncertain and alternatives are accepted, then either Christ has failed in his purpose, in his promises, and is not God or God himself has failed to keep his word with men. Either way the Christian faith becomes vain. But thanks be to God his Word endures and if we cannot like St. John see his glory, we can still hear his voice.

# III

# On Laughter

It was a man tempted to melancholy who wrote: "There's nothing worth the wear of winning, but laughter and the love of friends." Light-hearted laughter, yes: gentle amusement, yes: and if laughter were the same as being merry, then heaven should resound with laughter, for it is the place of endless joy. Medieval spiritual writers sometimes used the image of sitting at table with God and making merry. To be merry, however, is almost the same as to be joyous; not all joy is accompanied by laughter. Indeed, many good people hesitate to think of Christ laughing. Somehow or other laughter does not seem to them to fit in with the suffering majesty and compassion of Christ.

Why is this? An obvious answer is that laughter can so often be loud and boisterous or empty, and usually it is a release for men and women who are kept down or live on too tight a rein. But not all laughter is of this sort, for it can go with youth and innocence, is found in the happiest of homes and can even accompany great suffering. Psychologists offer various explanations of laughter. Most regard it as a form of compensation or as an overflow of high spirits and they see its immediate cause in the response to the incongruous. Man's dignity is such a silly thing that when he puts on airs he provokes laughter, and pride has a fall. Those who have lived among savages tell us that their laughter is cruel, and I have seen a child fall from a tree and the silent watchers only cackle with laughter. Our own ancestors not so long ago found amusement in watching brutal sports and human executions.

Is there then no place for laughter in the gospels and in the kingdom of God now and hereafter when we are once more embodied? God forbid! "Dost thou think, because thou art virtuous, there shall be no more cakes and ale?" We have in Sir Thomas More a saint who could joke and laugh even on the scaffold; and there is the enchanting story of the Syrian monk who, though dead, sat up laughing on his bier three times before burial because God so loved him and his fellowmen. Christ may well have teased Philip before the distribution of the loaves and fishes; and in the scenes after the Resurrection the laughter of peace and joy is never far off. In heaven's perpetual springtime, laughter will mingle with the recollections and renewals at the heavenly love feast.

# IV

# Development
# of Doctrine

The Gospels and the creeds are full of great images of Fatherhood and Sonship of the most high Lord who descends into Hell. These images help to unveil for us the mysteries of the Christian faith. Occasionally critics within or without the faith say we must needs get rid of them. Nowadays however it is not so much the images as the wording of Christian doctrine which has been coming under fire. The language, we are told, is outmoded because it has been borrowed from some musty philosophy; we must perforce learn to distinguish between the original divine message and the all-too-human, and often out-of-date, form in which it is expressed.

There is certainly a distinction between the Word of God and the philosophy in which it may be expressed. No system of philosophy has a divine guarantee. Nevertheless it is not easy to make a sharp separation. When the Fathers at Ephesus declared that Christ the Word was of one nature with the Father, they used philosophical language to make clear what was divinely revealed. What the theologians in the early centuries sought was to find words which would be both intelligible and acceptable. They looked around for the best thought of their time and made it their servant. The systems of philosophy they used may not have been flawless; much of it may sound antiquated, but its value lay in making people see the original truth better.

Does not this, however, suggest that from the very beginning there was a fully fledged truth — and theologians could turn to it for verification as we can test the likeness in a portrait by turning to the original man or woman? Such a view would seem neither sound nor historical, for true growth is not an accident, and the development of a doctrine is not just the adornment of something which remains as fixed and immobile as a stone. St. Peter, let us say, when he heard

24

from heaven the definitions of the Councils would have clapped his hands in recognizing that here was true growth where there is both identity and change. St. Peter, for instance, certainly had the advantage of seeing the Lord, but every age by faith has the evidence for the same Lord and the same truth and the advantage of a growing or grown faith. But how can we be sure that we are not defecting from the original news? What criterion have we in adopting new philosophical expressions. I know of no answer to this question unless the Pauline conception of the Church be accepted. If the Church be the new Body of Christ of which he is the Head, then its age-long consciousness has an identity, as each individual has a unique sense of who he is and what he thinks. The Holy Spirit in the Church keeps truth one and the same down the ages all the while it presides over its growth. "We live the truth in love and so grow up in Him who is our Head, Christ."

# V

# The Coming of Christ

As Christmas draws near the Church dwells lovingly on the picture of God made man, of God a child as helpless as all children are. This is a birthday feast, but it is more than that, for the Church has also in mind the truth of Christ's continuous presence and His Second Coming. In a way the First Coming and the Second Coming run together, for Christ is both Alpha and Omega. The Second Coming, it is true, has a special mission of its own, for He will "come again to judge the living and the dead;" but as He showed Himself to His Mother and His foster-father and the shepherds, and enlightened the Magi, so He is addressing human beings and knocking at their doors in all ages and in every place until the end of time. He called the Apostles, He cured the sick, He brought Mary Magdalen back to true love, He looked longingly at the rich young man — and the two disciples recognized Him in the breaking of bread at Emmaus. So too we encounter Him, though not visibly.

What special form then, if any, does this meeting take? The Gospel is the announcement of good news, and the good news is Christ Himself, the Word and the Life. The Gospel gives us a further clue when it insists on crises and special moments of grace or opportunities. It is on these occasions especially that we can enter into that dialogue of love which will be consummated in eternity.

If this be so, then Christ is as alive now and present as before in Galilee and in Jerusalem; only He is hidden. He is now hidden in His Members and in His Sacraments and is as one "slain but alive." He reigned from a Cross and triumphed through death. Hence He is more likely to be met where the Cross is. We are told in the Gospels to be ever ready, loins girt and lamps in our hands, for His coming is unexpected and dark like that of a thief in the night. The foolish virgins were unprepared; they had no oil, and they missed the great occasion; the doors were closed upon them. Amongst much else that Christmas tells us is its reminder of the presence of God in the world, offering us a new birth, a new marvellous perfection; and we can never be sure when He will greet us and ask us for proof of our loyalty and love.

# VI

# God and Evil

A favorite distinction at the moment is that of *existential* and *essential*. The *existentialist* insists that life is more than mind or thought (there is not a sneeze in Hegel's system); we must meet experience at first hand, head on, and not just with the ideas made up in our head. Man must commit himself, take decisions, take even his life in his hands and prove himself "authentic." The essentialist stays with ideas and systems of thought and equates thought with reality. The distinction all must admit needs careful handling, for if we run way from thought we are lost. Reason saves us from bogus answers and from the asylum.

Nevertheless, this distinction helps us to

keep a right balance, and it helps us to feel our way, for instance, in the problem of evil. All know from experience what evil is, whether moral or physical, and we read of it every day. So badly are many hurt by it that they ask how can there be a good God behind the human scene? The philosopher may, perhaps, tell them that evil precludes the possibility of there being a God. Now when the philosopher talks or argues in this way he is being an "essentialist." He assumes that human reason is omnicompetent and that man can see so clearly into the mystery of God, "whose ways are not as our ways and whose thoughts are not as our thoughts." At one moment he says that God is a meaningless idea or unknowable, and at the next he writes as knowing the secret divine counsels.

The truth is that with our mortal eyes we cannot see the sun of God's justice. We have enough knowledge to trust Providence, but not comprehend it. Moreover we seem to grow in freedom by overcoming evil. Our growth is by tension, by venture and in arduous days and by self-sacrifice, so that it is next to impossible to disentangle joy and sorrow, the good from the bad. I believe philosophy can bring an understanding of

God's ways which insures peace of mind. But, in fact, it is the existential answer which God has provided to enlighten our ignorance and summon us to joyous hope. God has not supplied us with a full intellectual answer, still less with an apologia. He has done something better: He has entered into our human experience, for Calvary witnesses to God as so much in love with Man as to die for him. No longer can we harbor the suspicion that God is indifferent to our suffering or that He chose the world lightly, seeing that it has involved the agony and death of God himself.

# VII

# Joy in Knowledge

One who is always right makes a poor companion. He is even more irritating than a bore. Why this should be is not easy to say. As a child I thought happily that my father knew everything, and at school I enjoyed the master whom no question could silence or baffle. I suppose that as we grow up we grow more sensitive to our shortcomings and we like neither to be found ignorant nor to be eclipsed in knowledge. Besides, in self-defense we have to think of the too-learned man as dull, smug or conceited. If, however, we look further into this matter of universal learning, we must acknowledge that at times encyclopaedic persons are a blessing; they are the outriders of one who knows all and inscribes it with love. Such mounting knowledge must have a summit from which all can be seen.

I doubt if we now esteem wisdom as much as in other times and in more eastern lands. Once the talk turns to what is beyond and above the practical, most of the company lose interest. Even the prayers and forms of Christianity in West and East here show a difference. Santa Sophia at Constantinople is only the greatest among many churches dedicated to Wisdom in the East, and Orthodox thinkers have foretold a third glorious period of Christianity guided by the Holy Spirit.

Wisdom demands a quiet, contemplative spirit. The rush of modern life, the commuting to and from the cities, the speed of travel, and the constant assault on our senses are not conducive to even a philosophical calm. Universities multiply, but it is the technical arts and sciences which are stressed. So great is the strain of city life that men and women take refuge in the country to find the cure for nerves and fretfulness and nagging thoughts. From bees and flowers and the call of birds at sunset the mind comes to a deeper heart and enters into the movement of nature and the seasons. Quietly knowledge accumulates. Better for us, however, than nature would it be to have the One who made nature take us by the hand and show us the inscape of each object and its purpose in a providential world. The Apostles as they walked through the fields and valleys with Christ must at times have felt how all around reflected the Creator and took on a new beauty. They were growing wise despite themselves, and like Shadrach, Meshach and Abednego, cried out upon all things to praise the Lord.

# VIII

# Flesh and Spirit

St. Paul tells us of the way the flesh can war against the spirit, and we ourselves are only too conscious of our divided self. This is shown in our loving, for there is a semi-animal love, which has often little to do with reason, and has its seasons and moments. It rises and falls, and after the fall the object of our desire can be a twenty years' removed thing. We are lucky in having such a love, and it can give zest and exhilaration to a higher form of loving which we also know to be ours. This latter however can do without the first and be efficacious, all passion spent.

Proper human love normally requires the liaison of the two, but at times the lusting urge is out of place. When St. Augustine tells us of his evening with his mother, St. Monica, near Ostia shortly before she died, and of how in the love and unity of their soaring thought they fell silent, we see a side of human life which separates man entirely from the animal and brings him nearer to the angel. How inadequate a picture of man it is to consider him as no more than animal! A human but truly spiritual love is felt when we enter into the suffering of others in far distant parts of the world or in past times, or again in the presence of death, when one we love can no longer speak to us. Great souls are not limited by time or space or family or nation in their love; no one in distress of mind or body is outside their care. It is this generosity of spirit which strikes us in St. Paul's cry: "Who is hurt and I am not hurt?" And it is most completely represented by Christ in the Garden of Gethesemane and on the Cross, where a God-man could thirst for souls with a body transfixed by pain and dried up with loss of blood.

# IX

# Our Unchanging God

God, as the theologians tell us, is so perfect that He is incapable of change. The idea comes out of Greek thought, which maintains that the more perfect a being is the greater its vitality, its resistance to death, decay or any change. Change is the mark of what is finite, of what might not be — and all such imperfection must be set aside when we contemplate Almighty God. "All things are passing, He alone remaineth"— and we should be grateful that God has created us in love and that His love for us is unchanging.

When we turn to the Bible we are confronted with a God who is perfect in all ways, but the language is not of an immutable and necessary being: Yahweh "has care of us,"

He is our Father, a supremely free personal being. How then reconcile these two accounts with their different emphases? We can profit by meditating on both, and without question the mystics tend to use the language of immutability — God is the plenitude of being, the unchanging ocean of deity. Yet we learn more from the Gospels, for we can relinquish our inadequate ideas and meet a Presence; we are drawn by love of Another, and this love promotes a new understanding.

A friend of mine thought of God as a never-ceasing blaze or radiation of love; and all change is on our side, for such love looks like, and even is, justice and anger as it meets evil and repercusses in us. But I do not feel that this explains the quite personal love of Our Father and of the Son who quit His equality with the Father for our sake. Somehow all the value of unchanging perfection does allow for the personal love between the Father and the Son and for Christ's love, which joins us in Him with the Father through the suffering of the Cross.

# X

# On Freedom

Of freedom there are many sorts. We speak of freemen, who are no longer slaves or in contrast with prisoners. Here the sense is freedom from physical restraints imposed by man or even by nature, as when we rejoice in being free of sickness or crutches. Karl Marx thought that the essence of freedom lay in a consciousness of necessity. His point was that the savage is at the mercy of nature, whereas civilized man, becoming conscious of nature's laws, the workings of tides, gases, electricity and nuclear power, can harness them to his needs. Better, however, surely, to call this freedom the power of option among known necessities.

It is plain that our freedom works in and through and amid necessities. We cannot jump over the moon, nor put back the clock, nor swim the Atlantic. We behave exactly like a Druid or King Cambyses. Each of us is limited by body and inheritance: what we are given, that we have to develop and adorn. Freedom here lies in choice, in the power to say yes or no, to plan and to act, to fashion and spread loveliness out of the material provided to us. This power can dwindle or increase; it dwindles all too easily as we shirk responsibility or by indulgence grow enslaved to a habit or passion: it grows with wise use, and various ingenious practices of West and East prove that we can acquire an extraordinary control over our brains and minds.

It is of this latter freedom that spiritual writers have much to say. True liberty for them means freedom from sin, the emancipation from servitude to our body and our passions. They do not stop at the ideal of our being masters of ourselves, for we can still use our liberty to seek power over others. The highest liberty is to be found in giving, in the adoption of the ideals which God prescribes and which Christ exemplified on a cross of love. Imitation here passes into identity with the highest. The soul encounters a living God of love and finds itself anew, possessor of itself and all it could dream of.

# XI

# The New Name

It was commonly believed in ancient times that each person had a secret name, and this name was his passport to reality. If an enemy could know and possess it he would thereinafter take possession of the other. This superstition arose from misunderstanding a profound truth. Each of us has a unique selfhood, and the "I" of the first person should be the very expression of who we are, intimately and really. Our secret name is the personality as given to us and intended for us by God. This name, however, is partly hidden from us, and indeed it is a name which has still to be articulated. Our life consists in writing our name, in making our mark that singular, indelible and creative mark, whatever our position in life, however undistinguished in the world's eyes we may be. Here is our life's pursuit, to make our name, in solitude always but also as citizens within the gay, sad community being re-formed in Christ.

We are given names at birth, and if we are Christians we are christened with a name which makes us one of the family of Christ. Our name spreads out in marriage; the wife changes her maiden name to take on a new one. This changing is a symbol of the mysterious destiny of our own selves, and of the everlasting coat of arms first won for us by Christ. We can darken and disgrace our name; we can fail to be what God has meant us to be, becoming idle pretenders, a Dives who has no spiritual substance or a Peer Gynt who has never lived, mere Pirandello phantoms.

Plaese God we may come to realize our true name as a new name in Christ; for he possesses the many-splendored beauty of our human nature, and we serve to exhibit some hitherto unmanifested trait of it, as we walk co-consciously with Him through life.

# XII

# Good Sense in Religion

There are few, if any, particular moral principles or virtues which provide a single thoroughfare from earth to heaven. Courage we need, and kindness and frankness, but we have always in practicing them to exercise what is now called common or good sense, and by the ancients prudence or wisdom. There are occasions when it is hard to be sure whether severity should precede kindness or not, and discretion bravery. So long as we live we shall need to call on that good sense or power of judgment which enables us to make the right decisions, to refrain from overpressing a claim or being too frank with a nervous invalid. We are constantly in danger of being insensitive to the varying troubles of those we meet, of asking too little from the high-spirited and too much from those hurt in life by ugly homes, poor schooling or bad habits.

Now this may sound bourgeois or uncreative to ardent souls, and even look like worldliness in the light of the folly of the saints, who gave their all for love. (Today much is said and written about "commitment" and naked, daring faith.) Is love the great exception to the rule I have laid down? It appears so, for the lover does despise half-measures and is never content save in giving himself and all he has to the beloved. Love breaks all rules, let us admit, and comes the nearest to a simple rule of life. But this language of "folly" and "madness" will not do, and love also may need discretion; as when the bear, seeeing the fly on its sleeping master's nose, seized a paving stone to strike it dead and leave his master sleeping. True love is not so much a madness as an identification of self with the other, and this means that there is a kind of higher good sense which tells the lover what the other wants and would have him do. In the case of God we must learn his ways and wishes, remembering the injunction, "If you love me keep my commandments." Here then good sense is still required, but at this level it reaches up to being an understanding love, wisdom, in fact, which corrects love's frenzies.

# XIII

# The Cross Is Our Hope

Ancient Greek thinkers for a time brooded over change, asking themselves how a thing could be the same and not the same from moment to moment. Parmenides concluded that all change must be an illusion; another philosopher, a great man, said that nothing ever remained the same. An object like a taper aflame and self-consuming was his best explanatory image. We still debate the matter. I expect some of us remember our amazement as children on being told that the ugly duckling turned into a swan and a grub into a butterfly.

With the discovery of Evolution interest in the problem revived, and not only as regards physical living things. How, it was asked, can

51

abiding truths, natural and revealed, also grow? An answer here was imperative if, as Christians believed, men lived in the light of a divine Revelation given nearly two thousand years ago. The usual answer given is that what is implicit can become explicit. This view without some tests such as Newman's, namely, permanence of type and continuity of principle, would leave Christian doctrine at the mercy of an Abelard. More in the way of explanation seems needed, and so Newman added "a power of co-ordination making for a chronic vigor."

This may help us to judge the difference in the past between true and false developments. So great, however, is the change in cultural climates and in outlooks in various times and parts of the world that, even as Shakespeare's text will prompt new interpretations from an eighteenth-century critic in England and France and from a twentieth-century critic in America and Germany, so the Gospel, while containing the same message for all, will unveil itself anew in every age. In this sense we keep arriving afresh at an understanding of God and the mysteries of faith. Moreover, the Christian Church believes in the assistance of the Holy Spirit. Christ is with his Church all days even to the

end of time. The Church is the extension of
Christ, his Mystical Body; so just as a man
who knows himself can read his own mind,
the Church looks to its Lord and Head and
interprets his mind with love and certainty.

Blessed are they who have no expectations for they will not be disappointed. This
ninth beatitude, as it has been called, is like
a cold douche on those who look forward
to a perfect society here on earth. " 'Excel-
sior!' he cried and fell into a ditch." No
Christian can be cynical or pessimistic, for
it is of faith that God has loved man enough
to die for him. Such redemptive love inspires
hope, and now that all peoples of the earth
are reaching a grown-up stage and knowledge grows apace, many respond to the vision of a Teilhard de Chardin — a vision of a
time when the human race will be united by
knowledge and love. The Ecumenical Coun-
cil breathed the same spirit of hope and
prayed that enmities might die down and
controversies turn into rewarding dialogues.

Peace therefore on earth is the concord
of mind and heart. Yet, when we read the
papers or listen to our neighbors, we learn
of little to encourage us: strikes expressing

distrust, parties inveighing against each other, race troubles, and nations building walls of separation or invading territories not theirs by right. Add to this the daily gossip about family quarrels, libels, robberies, murders, the savage words of youth and the cynicism of age. How is all this to be smoothed away: how shall "the crooked be made straight and the rough places plain?" Some fall back on the saying that God writes straight with crooked lines; others believe in a Limbo where the mind and heart can be reformed and re-educated in the school of divine love; others again accept all the opposition to good, declare it be a law of life, a view which has been worked up by Heraclitus, Hegel and Marx.

Of these solutions, the last presents a problem and a kind of answer intelligible to a scientific mind. It means that we accept the fact of evil from the very beginning of history pitted against the good. Species have evolved by a struggle for existence into higher forms. Without a struggle organic functions degenerate, and in the Biblical account of man salvation came finally after man had disobeyed God, brother had killed brother, and the true prophets had been exiled or stoned by their people. The child goes reluctantly to school, the grown-up has to fight temptation within and without. In fact the sign of advance in true living, the sequel of hope, is the Cross. Optimism, then, is justified insofar as man meets his opportunity and accepts the challenge, and so grows unselfish and closer in mind and spirit to his neighbor. In his own small way each individual can say, "I being lifted up will help to draw all men around a Cross."

# XIV

# On Obedience

There is much stir nowadays in theological circles about the meaning of obedience. Why and when should a person yield himself and accept commands? The new argument or questioning is supplied by one of the new schools of philosophers. They dislike all that is impersonal, the treatment of another human being as a thing. Only an I-Thou relationship is fitting between two or more persons. A person has inviolable rights; he stands on an equality with all others, and his full consent must be asked and given whenever he is called upon to obey. Some theologians, with their minds on the tradition of vows and promises and hierarchical powers, try to reinforce this new view by pointing out that the Christian religion is essentially one of love (Caritas), and therefore no command can be genuine and acceptable which does not follow from the all-embracing ultimate principle of Charity.

Now the propounders of this view would, I am confident, allow for exceptions in times of emergency and dire stress. With such emergencies in mind certain bodies of men and women are trained to respond immediately and without question to an order. "Their's not to reason why." Battle is such an emergency ,and so too are all those threats from storms and floods and fires and whenever the saving of lives has to be prompt. Imagine a great surgeon being challenged at a critical moment of an operation. But once this is admitted, it is hard to draw the line, for throughout life situations arise which need common action and a leader. May it be that this view is an attempt to express an ideal, one which is workable only among wise and highminded men and women? In our ordinary life, in the home and at school as well as in businesses and professions, goodwill with discipline seems ordinarily to work better than goodwill by itself. A reasonable obedience is practical and less idealistic, and should always be aimed at

58

between persons and in societies. In a state, to take one example, the people should use their judgment in choosing their government, and should also from then on give them a willing service. Only on serious matters of conscience ought the private individual to be given congé. In a Christian society there is, as the new school emphasizes, a special principle of love, but such a love is in danger of overdoing obedience, because the lover wants to give all, holding nothing back. Obedience in the context of Christ is just another word for Caritas.

# XV

# Still Small Voice

Guns are fired on royal and great occasions and bands play and people shout. Even the Russians do more than smile enigmatically; they clap hands at parades and in greeting heroes. In contrast with these human manfestations many religions, and those of the highest, enter into an intense silence at the most solemn moments, as witness the Eleusinian mysteries and the rites of Isis and Mithra and our Western Eucharist.. "The Lord is in his holy temple: let all the earth keep silence before him." These are the moments when the creature feels the presence of a goddess or the true God and hides within that immensity. For special occasions, when a tribe or group has to be alerted to some divine message or advent, at events such as the death of the Son of God or the birth of the Church at Pentecost, sound is needed. But in a divinely established ceremoney where man meets God, a moment of silence is fitting as well as dramatic. "Be still and know that I am God."

In keeping with this, the great sacrament of the Church is called a mystery, for mystery originally meant a closing of the lips — the hush that falls in a supreme moment. Here we can see the efficacy of silence, and what holds for a public act of worship provides a lesson for the individual in his relations with God. God speaks in a still small voice to the soul, so small that any noise of creatures can distract from it. *Sileant creaturae, silentium est Christus*, which, if it must be turned into the vernacular, means "Let creatures be still, for the silence is Christ." That is why those who would keep pure of heart and work so that God's will may be done as it is in heaven withdraw at times into silence, that like Mary the Mother of God they may keep all his sayings in their hearts.

In and by nature we can learn of God, and still better from our neighbors; but God has secrets to reveal to every individual, and each must train himself to listen. Here perseverance is necessary. It may be easy to be silent on a peak in Darien, but the Pacific is only a drop of water compared to God's intimate immensity. The world is well lost for a moment of such intimacy — the world, that is to say, which is noisy and confusing.

# XVI

# On Holiness

Saints are said to be difficult to live with, and there is some truth in the saying if it means that they bring home to us our own shallow conceits, our selfishness and second-rate ideals. The near-saint is often shunned because he can be angular, ruthless and insensitive to the feelings of others, and even the true saint may be an uncomfortable companion. St. Thomas à Becket was too inflexible for his king; St. Francis of Assisi gave little thought to comfort or good food; St. Peter Claver, in his devotion to the black slaves, did not mind dirt or bad smells. The nearer, however, their image comes to that of Christ the more winning they become.

If we ask ourselves what we mean by holiness, the ready answer is the imitation of Christ or being "perfect as your heavenly Father is perfect." But this does not explain how there are so many different types of sanctity nor the different stresses which are to be found as new attitudes to human nature develop. A hermit and probably a pure contemplative, I was assured recently by a group of Christian young men and women, is not a genuine Christian. The Christian ideal is a fellowship and must be sought in common human enterprises. Is this a passing phase or a new sense of the part Christians have to play in the world? I wonder whether such neighborly zeal will bear much fruit if we cease to commune with the invisible God as Christ did at night? If we neglect prayer and the study of the saints we may find that we have little to give our neighbor; we may become competent social workers, nurses and earnest politicians but not saints.

Holiness is the one thing necessary, and it is not too hard to recognize. Christ is walking or talking with us in another person's stride or voice. More specifically the marks of it, I should say, are unselfish affection and genuine humility. The saint has no illusions about himself and is not easily offended. He is shy of praise of himself but glad to praise others, and he is never prevented by self-conceit from doing what is best in God's interest and his neighbors'. This fearless humility opens his soul for God's entry and co-conscious presence. His mind widens and grows more sympathetic to all God's creatures. Even when thinking of his enemies or persecutors the words attributed to Christ by a medieval poet re-echo in his mind, "Come on, my friend, my brother most entire; For thee I offered up my blood in sacrifice."

# XVII

# Answers to Prayer

Scientists have been questioning the efficacy of prayer — the prayer of petition, that is — and they have been, as might be expected, unable to detect constant notable results from it. I think they should exclude special cases, places and occasions, such as Lourdes or the miracles examined for the canonization of a saintly person or martyr. Here there is plenty of apparent evidence, and that is why sceptics are at such pains to disprove the evidence or reduce it. Normally, however, answers to prayer are not of the kind which could be proved in court. There are cases of remarkable recoveries, escapes from danger, strange coincidences. We can pray for so many things, for those dear to us, for ourselves and for causes which we have at heart, for the poor and suffering all over the world, and for peace. Usually we cannot be quite sure that our prayer brought about the asked for result, and it would be silly to pretend to certainty. As a nurse said to mas as a child, when I complained that cod-liver oil was not doing me any good, "Just think what you would be like if you had not been taking it." Such an answer would not please a scientist or logician, but in a dialogue with a loving God we do not need their approval.

Going a little deeper into this matter, we know that God is not in time, and that he has not to be awakened from sleep by our importunity, even though the Gospel does use this imgae. The Gospel tells us to pray to Our Father who will give us all that is for our good. God eternally knows our petitions, and therefore they do not come as something new to him. It may well be that praying is good for us, primarily because we are all one family and it would be inhuman not to be concerned. There is a mystery here of divine Providence, I confess, but pragmatically we can see that there may be a conflict between what we ask and God's dispositions for us and others. In the Garden of Gethsemane, Christ asked that the cup should be taken from him, but added, "not my will but thine be done." This second clause is implicit in all our prayers, and in truth the cup Christ drank has brought hope and salvation to innumberable souls. Again, when laid on the Cross he prayed for his executioners, "Father, forgive them, for they know not what they do." We can wait confidently for the after-life to show the benefit of this great prayer for all who have crucified him in thought or act.

# XVIII

# The Supernatural

The Christian meaning of the word "super-natural" tends to be lost in the indiscriminate modern use of it. It is now more often that not associated, if not identified, with the superstitious or the preternatural or the odd. Any event which at first defies explanation is called supernatural until it is explained away. Hence spooks, poltergeists, second-sight and paranormal phenomena are all classed together under this word. This kind of use has been abetted by the steady advance of scientific knowledge of natural processes and the human brain. What was once assumed to be miraculous is now often explicable in medical terms, and the result has been a sceptical attitude to supernatural claims. This scepticism is now shared by certain groups of theologians. They agree that in past ages when people were ignorant of science and more childish it was natural to appeal constantly for help to God and to suppose that God constantly gave special help. The supernatural world was as credible to them as Santa Claus to a child. But now man has come of age and must dispense with all these ancient and artificial aids to living. Religion must give up its mythology and become one with the secular world which is man's habitat.

This supposed coming of age, however, itself can come close to being a myth. In some degree man has become more independent, resourceful and competent, but not so as to feel liberated by leaving God out. Life as "a tale told by an idiot signifying nothing" has become the common refrain of modern literature and art. Our present-day mood is one of disappointment or fatuity, of *cris de coeur* and of horror at the prospect of death which stultifies all progress. The gospel of good news routed the ancient pessimism. The sting of death was removed, failures and misunderstandings could be remedied and evil turned into a good by redeeming love. The story of the king and the

74

beggar maid, the myth of Eros and Psyche, had revealed the dream of man, but the reality far exceeded the dream. "Ye shall be as gods." Human nature was wedded with the godhead, and this new springing, everlasting life defines the meaning of the supernatural.

# XIX

# The Good News
# of Easter

In Eastertide the first act of those who believe the Christian Creed will be one of adoring joy at Christ having risen from the dead, an act of joy more profound than that felt by Martha and Mary at the restoration to life of their brother Lazarus. Following this must come a second act, one of thanksgiving that we should be so privileged as to share in Christ's resurrection, both bodily and spiritually. "I am the Resurrection and the life; he who believes in me will live on." The truth of Christianity rests on the fact of the resurrection. If Christ be not risen, as St. Paul wrote, our faith is vain. Those who assume that genuine Christianity can by-pass this fact or omit it are like those simple folk in China who used to swallow the paper prescription of the doctor taking it to work like the real medicine. They may have a private religion of their own, but it is not Christianity.

We depend on what happened on the first Easter morning for the essential Christian virtues; for faith, "the substance of things hoped for," means the beginning of eternal life in Christ now for us. "I no longer live, Christ lives in me"; for hope, because He that is risen is in us and for us, and thereby we are given the sure promise of everlasting happiness; and for love, because He that is in us and for us and with us creates a new society of agapé, of which the symbol is the union of flesh and spirit in marriage. This society of love is created for us in the passion, death and resurrection of God made man; for He descends that we may ascend and share in God's life. Let us salute then once again "Our Lord Jesus Christ, raised from the dead, that great Shepherd whose flock was bright with the blood of an eternal covenant."

# XX

# On Snobbery

At a time when democracy is hailed as the ideal form of society, and the form which it tends to take is egalitarianism, to be a snob is the unforgiveable sin — and, to judge from remarks in word and writing, the commonest. In this matter it is easy to be inexact and unfair. The man who consorts with the rich and influential is not necessarily a snob; he may be a go-getter making friends with the mammon of iniquity. The snob is one who has a false sense of values with regard to family or position, and admires others or despises them by this criterion. Hence a man proud of his riches who despises others on that account is a snob. So too the sycophant who worships him out of all proportion. But Sir Godfrey Kneller was not a snob because he rated his artistic talents so high as to think he could have made a better job of the world than almighty God. Still less is the man or woman, be he statesman, artist, general or writer, who is aware of the excellence of his work. Furthermore it is salutary to esteem one's family, its name and the traditions and virtues of one's country; so too we have to wish well of those appointed by God to look after us.

The trouble with snobbery is that it insinuates itself so easily into our outlook. We are so prone to live on false values and to seize opportunities of scoring over others. That means constant pretence on our part — hiding what is shameful and telling tall stories about our exploits, our relationships, our circumstances. In the Gospels there are genealogies of Christ, giving his descent from King David. There is the example of the publican Zacchaeus whom Christ liked for his honesty. Snobbery dies in the presence of Christ, and we shall feel far from snob·· bish when Christ looks us through and through. It is good to praise others and to give due when honor is due, but for ourselves and for society the Christian standards of humility, unselfishness and wise discernment are the right ones to follow.

# XXI

# Our Abiding City

The writer of the Letter to the Hebrews tells us that "Jesus, who would sanctify the people through his own blood, suffered beyond the city gate," and he bids us "to go out to him away from the camp. For here we have no continuing city, but we seek one to come." This is the authentic declaration of our condition here on earth. There is no abiding city here in the natural order, and we are reminded of this truth as we pass the innumerable cemeteries or gaze upon the ruins — still often lovely — of past civilizations. Our time here is limited, and every minute of it is precious, enabling us to declare ourselves in terms of love and fitting acts. In God's intention each of us has a work to do building the new Jerusalem, work apportioned to the unique beings we are. And it is here the world's standards give us little help, for the apparently infinitesimal opportunities offered to us may have more creative effects for good than all that is contained in the brave talk of the mighty or applauded in the press or on the radio.

There are those now who tell us that Christianity must be secularized, but they know not what they say or do. A secularized religion would once more hammer the nails into the hands and feet of God. What is natural turns unnatural without grace. The way needs be narrow that leads to life, and it is uphill. In this world labor and sacrifice are our lot, with the great contentment of doing the will of God from day to day, and seeing love light up the faces of those dear to us, of those who share our work, and the stranger and the poor. It is in this way that we go out of the city to an altar, and in return find that 'round that altar all that was fair and honorable in the city is to be found even more abundantly.

# XXII

# A Luminous Mystery

Those who are anxious to know more about God should turn to the revelation of the Holy Trinity and the work of the Holy Spirit within it. Is this not the unique clue to the mystery of God (and much else, a light upon what infinite loving and infinite being must be like)? The problem of God, so to call it with all reverence, is being proclaimed nowadays from the housetops not only of atheist but also of official religious dwellings. Divinity schools are not ashamed of denying their own right to exist by declaring that God is dead. Their proclamation may be a cry of the heart; it is also an avowal that in the presence of modern knowledge and techniques God cannot be found.

God is said to be "totally other." If so, it is asked, how can any description fit him? Again, God is not verifiable by the senses: he is strangely silent and he seems to take no part in a world which is called his creation. These and many other objections are felt strongly by some *avant-garde* theologians. They ignore the long debates of the past conducted by intellectual geniuses and saints, which did in effect provide a language in which to address God. They ignore too the universal witness of the past in prayers, works of art and buildings which show how indissolubly man is connected with God. Religion is man's climate as the body is the focus of the soul and the air the lens through which we see objects. God is unavoidable, more necessary than the air, more intimate than our own body; he is the living source of our conscience. That is why those who create a silence within themselves and an empty space hear his voice and know his presence. But such subconscious knowledge never satisfies, and we would gladly know more about God. May it not be that the final meaning of love is distantly given to us in the triadic movements of a love where the Father and the Son, though distinct, are lost in each other, and the in-betweenness is love again, the link of love between the Father and the Son? In such an exchange nothing is lost: all is gain, and personal life is a community, where there is full equality and complete freedom — love's plenitude.

# XXIII

# Exiles from Home

A friend of mine has written to me saying that to her the sense of "exile" in life is the best pointer to the truth and meaning of the Christian message. She will not mind my quoting her words about the "ineluctable sense of 'exile' which seems to haunt every century and each individual writer in turn. . . . No one could, I think, deny that the sense of 'exile' is there — 'The choked, lost feeling of being astray in the century like a small child in a strange alley.' But the child knows that home also exists." The conclusion from this is that man at the back of his mind is aware that he has a home and feels either that he has lost it or somehow is on his way to it — sometimes with joy as is told in the Psalms of the reapers who "go forth sowing in tears what they will reap one day with joy."

The theme here stated under the title of "Exile" is a perennial one — with variations, from the Cave of Plato to Ulysses *à la* Tennyson or Joyce. Each of us, if we do not at first recognize the theme in our experience, should go back carefully on our past recalling especially those thoughts in the silences of the night, the emotions accompanying our goodbyes, and the melancholy which follows extreme joys, when they pass, as all things pass. Is our life to be a series of successive, incomplete experiences which disappear, or are they the foreshadowing of what is to come and therefore meaningful because of it? St. Paul reminded his converts that they had not on earth an abiding city. The current religious bias is towards the temporal, the sanctifying of the secular as it might be called; but the specter of death prevents any hope of fulfillment here. Exile, however pleasant, is not home. We seek a better world, where all tears will be wiped away, and love will have no regrets or disappointments.

# XXIV

# Open-Eyed

Open-mindedness is an educational ideal, and rightly so if it be contrasted with narrowmindedness. It is our duty to remove motes, as well as beams, from our eyes, and we are called upon to face reality and not to shy away from it. Open-mindedness, however, has more than one sense. It may mean that we have a wider outlook than that of those around us — one which separates us from the herd or the conventionally accepted viewpoint. Our view is then our own, and, more than that, we see with a single eye and so approach that simplicity of the child which was praised by Jesus Christ. Such simplicity is not childish or naive; it clears away the prejudices, dislikes and fears which so often distort the judgments even of the educated. To behold the image of God in our neighbor, to prefer trust to suspicion, to distinguish between the genuine and the spurious, to see through the pretenses which hide reality from us and so see it for what it is — that is the prerogative of one who keeps or returns to the innocent look of the child.

Lastly, we can call open-eyed those who see with understanding and affection, and thereby are enabled to penetrate into truths and events more than those around them. The shepherd knows his sheep by name, the priest should see Peters and Magdalenes in the confessional; the good mother reads the faces of her children and enters into their joys and sorrows, and the beloved can keep few secrets from the lover. Love makes for sympathetic and even mystic understanding, an understanding which sees infinity in the palm of a hand and eternity in an hour. The crowd at Calvary just saw three men suffering for their supposed crimes, but the centurion saw a just man dying, and a Christian sees God redeeming. Such are among the advantages of being open-eyed.

# XXV

# Closed-Eyes

On seeing a blind man one is moved to compassion, and it seems a miracle of grace or nature that so often the blind appear content or even happy. It is, however, not compassion but distress which is aroused when one meets those who are mentally or spiritually blind. Life lived with open eyes is nature's panacea. We can grow only by seeing and facing reality, and those who retreat from truth into a world of illusion of their own become human failures. They may be as learned as Diogenes or as silly as Malvolio. Far better a rogue like Falstaff or a romantic like Don Quixote who, despite their follies, enjoyed God's good things.

# FACING THE PEOPLE

The mystics tell us that truth is in a well; so in certain cases it may happen that the sightless are not so badly off or so much less lucky than those who see. Indeed there is an old tradition, illustrated in ancient stories and plays, that the really wise must be blind. It is a Tiresias or a blind prophet who is listened to even by kings. They may have had a surfeit of ordinary sights and information and closed their eyes to seek within for what the spirit longs to possess. Withdrawal from outside traffic to the sanctuary of the soul is a necessary stage in the path to perfection. The initiations at the Eleusinian mysteries, in the worship of Isis and Mithras, took place in the dark. It is after the silence of prayer and discipline of the flesh that God is found within us, and we can listen for and hear his voice. Closed eyes are not necessarily a punishment or a fatal defect. "Be shellèd, eyes, with double dark and find the uncreated light."

# XXVI

# A Reasonable Obedience

True obedience is composed of duty and love. Children have duties towards their parents, and love makes them easy and even multiplies the obligations. So too in any community, be it one of labor unions, clubs, parties or nation. The true patriot feels bound to serve his country, and his love of it makes him willing, should the call come, even to suffer and die for it. Above all is this true in religion, where God our Maker and our end gives us a tenfold commandment, only that in the end our willing service should be transformed with love and by an extraordinary privilege be lifted into unending union and felicity.

Obedience at the moment tends to be out of fashion, for it is said to interfere with the growth of personal responsibility and choice. This kind of talk contains a lot of nonsense, for no society could exist without rules which have to be kept willy-nilly. There is, however, as usual a half-truth imbedded in this lopsided talk. Obedience rests ultimately on the demands of our nation on what is required for its true development. As children's foods, however distasteful, ensure a healthy growth, so too duties are directives towards an ideal manhood. As such they are reasonable, and it is good that we should learn by reasoning how they help us to be ourselves. Hence theoretically duties do not conflict with freedom; they purify and test it, and moral imperatives are our own interests disguised.

I wrote "theoretically" because in fact life is not acted out on a neat, steady plan. In any society the common good takes precedence over secondary human rights, and the individual has often to sacrifice himself without any return in this world. Then there are the times of crisis when governments, generals, headmasters and parents have to bypass explanations of orders and insist on their being carried out. Again, in a family and, above all, in a Christian community, love absorbs reason. In the Church Christ is the head and we are the members; he is the vine and we are the branches. Disobedience here would be like a cancerous growth in a body. Unity is another word for love for, as St. Paul says, "Living the truth in love, we grow up in Him who is our Head, Christ."

# XXVII

# Knowing God

St. Paul in his letter to the Romans exclaims: "How deep is the mine of God's wisdom, of his knowledge; how inscrutable are his judgments, how undiscoverable his ways! Who has ever understood the Lord's thought or been his counsellor?" In these words St. Paul is re-echoing the great prophets of Israel as well as writing out of his own experience. He realizes how impotent human language is to describe the divine majesty, and truth is better expressed in words and praise, which in turn may pass into ecstasy.

This is far from a modern view that God must be treated as dead and religion from now on should restrict itself to finding the divine in one's neighbor. All true religion begins in awe. The shadow and reflections of God stir in us the only right attitude and gives us a sense of God as beyond scrutiny, beyond comparison and beyond all our finite images. Moses is the prototype of all who encounter the true God — where before his Creator the creature feels fear and trembling love. The human and the divine do not meet except in such a relationship. Without this we cannot even begin to be wise about God — or about anything else.

It is in this climate of a perfection around and about us and beyond us that all creative work is done. By our body we are at home in the sensible world; by our spirit we belong to the world of absolutes. That is how and why the high-minded Pythagoras turned the physical world into mathematical symbols, why Plato saw all that is visible as participating in absolute truth, goodness and beauty, and why St. Thomas Aquinas in the end put aside his great treatises on God, calling them but straw in comparison with the visions vouchsafed to him. This climate, in which the spirit is at home, is one that opens out into eternity. It is one of wonder and intimations, promises and commitments, not of scepticism. Hence St. Paul was using its native language when he went on to say,

"All things find in Him their origin, their impulse, the center of their being: to Him be glory throughout all ages. Amen."

# XXVIII

# Man's Strength and Weakness

Is it just a coincidence that in an age of scepticism so many want to have their say on every topic conceivable and expect to be listened to? Attend in any public place and you will hear one man after another pronouncing confidently on religion, politics, games, world affairs and the concerns of his next-door neighbor. I suppose one could have heard something of the same kind of talk in pre-Christian days in a Greek agora or Roman forum, but then the world was not so vast and complicated as now, nor was knowledge so technical and scientific. Then most believed in the power of the mind; now scepticism reigns, and it is fashionable to assert ignorance of God, humanity and the nature of the self. Is there then some connection between scepticism in high places and the opinionatedness of the populace? Robbed of ideas on all ultimate questions, the simpler folk react by being vociferously dogmatic when given the chance. To keep their self-confidence they have to fall back upon some redoubt of the self. Impressing others is also a good restorative of self-confidence; or perhaps talking loudly and dogmatically serves to keep at bay the suspicion of being a hollow man or cigarette-smoking nonentity.

In the Christian philosophy every man is of inestimable value because he is created by God for a purpose. He has a name and a creative job specially reserved for him. His work counts; he is loved, and at curfew time his reward will come. This view begets and ensures self-confidence, but does not exaggerate it, because there is a balancing doctrine that man of himself now historically can do very little. If he trusts himself alone and relies on his own virtue he will have a fall. He needs the support and inspiration of others; he can find himself truly best in common enterprises and in self-sacrifice. Above all he stands in need of the grace of a living God, who is a present help and a final reward.

# XXIX

# The Plan of
# Redemption

The sequence of events after Easter form a pattern which is not always understood. The clue is that with his death Jesus Christ takes on a new role and a new body so as to make his redetmptive act universal and to continue to be with man in every generation until the end of time. The Ascension marks the triumphal return of the Son to the Father, the work he came to do gloriously achieved, and at the same time it marks the Lord's passover to another state.

A modern theologian has suggested that the Ascension can be compared to a royal coronation. The king or queen begins to reign immediately the former sovereign dies. With the Resurrection of Christ his new reign begins — the reign which means everlasting life to all who accept God and the restoration of all things in Christ. The official ratification, so to speak, of this and the reward are promulgated in the Ascension. The last dying cry of Christ on the Cross, however, was, "It is finished." The mission, that is, of Christ was accomplished in and at his death. The new reign begins, and the whole earth is now undergoing a change under the sway of its divine new Lord. The world becomes a divine milieu. Christ has descended even "into hell" to rescue those who awaited the redemption, bringing light even into the darkest places of the earth. The whole cosmos as a result, to use St. Paul's words, is reorientated to the godhead, being transformed so as to become part of thet mystery of Christ triumphant.

But this is not all. Christ in glory is, in that striking image of triumph, at the right hand of God the Father almighty: he is also now the Head of a new Body — born not at Bethlehem but in Jerusalem at Pentecost. Mankind is born again into his life, and through his new Body, the Church, he is present in every generation, speaks with every tongue known to man and offers him a kingdom without end, a union of bliss unending with God.

# XXX

# The Christ of The Apostles

Much new work has been done upon the Gospels; they have been cleaned up, demythologized and polished, and they are now said to be the expression of the collective consciousness of the Church of the first century. This for me is too like the play Hamlet without the Prince of Denmark. What has for long impressed others as well as myself is the unique, unrivaled character of the person the Gospels describe and it is this ineffaceable impression which Jesus Christ made on the Apostles and his friends which seems to make this new kind of exegesis relatively unimportant. It is what the modern philosophers call a "category mistake."

# FACING THE PEOPLE

The Apostles were Jews. Ingrained in them was a horror of polytheism. Yahweh was the one and only true God — a God too difficult and mysterious to admit of any descriptive words, too holy and majestic to allow of any comparison with what was human. What kind of being, then, could it have been who despite apparent failure, utter humiliation and a despicable death, could yet create the belief in him that he was one with God himself? St. Peter, for example, writing of the days which he spent in Christ's company, said that "We were eyewitnesses of his majesty. For he received from God the Father honor and glory, when there came such a voice to him from the heavens: 'This is my beloved son in whom I am well pleased' and this voice which came from Heaven we heard when we with him on the holy mount." (2 Peter 1:17-18) Again, the beloved disciple, the writer of the fourth Gospel, declares this being to be the Word that was God, the Shekinah, the Divine Presence in the Temple, who pitched his tent among us. He writes his Gospel that those who read it may believe that Jesus is the Christ, the Son of God, and "believing ye may have life through his name." Finally, St. Paul, the last of the Apostles who had persecuted the

Christians, was so overwelmed by his experience on the way to Damascus and by what he learned of Christ thereafter that he was liable, in his letters, to burst into a paean of praise of the "First Born before the Ages" of which a typical example is: "I am sure that neither death nor life, nor height nor depth nor any creature can separate us from the love of God, which is in Christ Jesus."

With these and so many other testimonies which could be quoted, it is superabundantly clear that the personality of Christ was unique and overpowering, so much so that those who knew of him and spoke of him would not dare to take liberties in writing of him. The so-called consciousness of the early Church was fixed by its belief that God had become man and that his words were more sacred than the Tablets Moses brought down from Mount Sinai. St. Peter warned his readers to take heed of the sure word of prophecy. How much more of the Divine Word himself! He wrote that "we have a more sure word of prophecy wherewith ye do well to take heed, as unto a light that shineth in a dark place until the day dawn and the day star arise in your hearts; knowing this first that no prophecy in Scripture is subject of private interpretation." He goes on so say that those who "gave us prophecy (how much more Christ's teaching) were men whom God had sanctified and carried away even as they spoke by the Holy Spirit."

# XXXI

# He Descended into Hell

In the Apostle's Creed we recite the following words: "He (Christ) descended into Hell." These words are both mysterious and rich in suggestion. No doubt they are connected with an early tradition to which St. Peter makes reference in his first letter. "It was in his spirit that he (Christ) went and preached to the spirits that lag in prison." The context shows that St. Peter had immediately in mind those who died in the days of Noah and the Ark. And "the long-suffering of God waited" for them. The Church, however, has seen this descent as the coming of good news to the departed of all ages, who could not have access to the Throne of God before the reconciling death of Christ.

What the good thief heard upon the Cross, the waiting spirits of the dead heard when Christ "harrowed Hell."

We learn from this action of the Son of God, the intention of God that the whole world — past, present and to come —should see its salvation in Him. His self-sacrifice for love of man was to have no limits and in line with a great number of Saints and Doctors of the Church and modern scholars such as Westcott and Benoit, we may extend it even to the whole cosmos. This is in accordance with one translation of St. Paul's words that Christ "led all captivity captive," for he also descended under the earth. "He that descended is the same that ascended far above all heavens that he might fill all things."

Christ's first mission (as he himself declared) was to the Jews. He was not sent except to "the sheep of Israel" because all that had been promised in the Bible story to the chosen people had to be fulfilled. But the loving intention of God did not stop there. The early Christians were slow to realize the width and depth of the charity of God. No food was to be called unclean and no race was to be so privileged as to exclude a general and cosmic redemption. The good news was to be preached to the ends of the earth. Redemption worked back as well as forward, enlightening those who lay in the shadow of death. They, too, were to have entry into a full life of which the name and food and reality would be Christ himself. As Ladislaus Boros has well said in his *The Moment of Truth*: "At the moment of Christ's death, the veil of the Temple was rent in two from top to bottom — the veil, that is, that hung before the Holy of Holies. For Jewish mysticism and subsequently in the Christian interpretation of this mysterious happening, the veil of the Temple represented the whole universe as it stands between God and Man." "The whole cosmos," he goes on to write, "opens itself to the Godhead, bursts open for God like a flower." And God, in His triumphant descent into the innermost fastnesses of the world, tears open the whole world and makes it transparent to God's light, makes it even a vehicle of sanctification.

# XXXII

# Providence and Equilibrium

New facts and surprises always await the student of nature. It is easy to think of life below that of man as mainly the massacre of the weak, those less fitted to survive. "Nature red in tooth and claw," as the Victorians described it. But now we know better. There is cooperation in ways hitherto unsuspected, with a resultant equilibrium which it may be unwise to upset. Lichen, for instance, is a combination consisting of one particular species of algae and another of fungus, and the great beauty of some lichen is due to the cooperation of the two coexisting forms, which survive together despite, cold, heat or dryness.

To take another example, divers in the depths of the sea have discovered that there are creatuers such as the Pederson shrimp, whose life consists in cleaning and aiding the fish which approach them. The shrimp is described in a book entitled *The Torch of Life* as having a transparent body striped with white and spotted with violet and with long antennae. It takes up a position in a kind of traffic center and, as fish come by, it stretches out its long antennae and sways its body to call the attention of the fish. The fish may then swim within an inch or two of the shrimp, stay still and allow its head and gill-cover to be cleaned. Injuries also are attended to, for the shrimp, so the narrator tells us, climbs aboard and moves rapidly over the fish to see if there is anything wrong. it pulls out parasites with its claws and cleans the injured spots. The fish keeps still and lets the shrimp operate on its back and sides. Then it opens its gill-covers to allow a search underneath them. Finally the shrimp enters and leaves the mouth of th fish. So much appreciated is the work of the shrimp (done without pay!), that the fish line up in crowds, taking their turn to be cleaned. That the work is serviceable and indeed needed is proved by the fact that when the shrimp was taken away, the number of the fish decreased.

This is such a Franciscan kind of story that it makes us reconsider some of our impressions about the ruthlessness of nature. It would seem that running through it there are, as in man, impulses to self-giving as well as to aggression and survival. A human society only flourishes when the ideal of personal freedom is conjoined with a strong sense of interdependence. We know only too well how in one type of society individual freedom is sacrificed to the interests of the supposed general welfare, while in another society individual freedom is so extolled that the common good is lost to sight. The mystical Body of Christ presents to us this ideal — so hard to attain in practice — where the two impulses go hand in hand and persons thrive in the atmosphere of self-giving.

# XXXIII

# On Suffering

In its sympathy with the working man and woman and in consideration of the strain of modern city life, the Church has mitigated many of the penances and mortifications of the past. Lent is no longer such a grim, penitential season, and the days of fasting and abstinence have almost disappeared. Modern life has a tempo which is bound to be a strain. (There are said to be over 500 psychiatrists in the one square mile of Beverly Hills.) Not that the Church has changed its view of human nature and its bias against self-indulgence and avarice. Penances may not be any longer imposed, but we are told to reflect seriously on ourselves and our imperfections, to seek remedies for the latter and to carry our cross courageously.

117

Christ our Lord on the cross is a reminder of the realities of human life, of its injustice and cruelty, of the pains and sorrows which at one time or another all of us have to meet. Physical hardship can serve at times as an anodyne for mental anxieties and upsets, and when we love our work, especially if it be for others, the burden involved becomes a joy. Moreover, we never know what we may be called upon to endure — ill health, material losses, betrayals, even the martyrdom which Peter learned from his risen Lord was to be his lot. On a dungeon wall of the Tower of London a martyr scratched: "By a painful passage one passeth to a pleasant port." In those days human nature could be cruelly tested. I was reading in the life of one of the martyrs how one day Robert Cecil was riding out of London with a friend, and he spoke of Robert Southwell, the priest and poet. He called him "a Goliath of fortitude." "They boast," he said, "about the heroes of antiquity, but we have a new torture which it is not possible for a man to bear. And yet I have seen Robert Southwell hanging by it, still as a tree-trunk, and none able to drag a word from his mouth." (They were trying to get out of him the names of other priests and of friends

118

with whom he had stayed.)

In every age there had to be "Goliaths of fortitude" and their number has ever grown under the tyranny of Nazis and Russian and Chinese Communists. The evidence is overwhelming of atrocious tortures not only of the body but also of the bind. St. Paul cried out: "Who is hurt and I am not hurt?" We who form one holy community in Christ must co-suffer with these heroic sufferers and help them with our prayers and self-denial. In so acting, we play our part in the great redemptive act of Our Lord, bring relief to those in agony of body and mind and help them to realize the words of St. Paul that "the sufferings of this life are as nothing with the joys to come."

# XXXIV

# Conscience

We hear much today about conscience, whether in religious discussions or in law courts or even in schools and universities. Its importance comes from the realization that it is the most intimate expression of what we are and what we feel we ought to be. It is our very self in action or rather ourself in determining how we should act. "Here I stand and I can do no other." Moreover, it concerns our own freedom and responsibility, it arises in us as a command. To refuse this command would be the final act of treason to the self and herald its dissolution.

This is the reason why so many fall back under claims of conscience against the demands of parents, governments or churches.

In former times, in ages of religious belief, conscience was often felt to be in some mysterious way the voice of God; and we have examples in history of men such as St. Augustine or Cardinal Newman, who sensed the very presence of God in the intimations of their consciences. Most of us, however, are less fortunate, and in these days when we no longer live in a Christian culture and the very existence of God is questioned, those who refuse obedience to a state or to social rules do so in the name of conscience without any reference to God or to a religious authority.

In thus relying on conscience as a sufficient justification in itself, they are partly right and partly wrong. We do not and should not think of conscience as identical with a command of God. A commandment presupposes that what is ordered is right and good. The commandment does not itself make the act good although we may have a duty to obey a justly constituted authority, such as parents or state, in all that is not sin. But clearly we must know what good and right are before we believe in God for we must know that God is good before we choose to obey him. But while this is so, we rely on conscience to our own peril if we do not give thought to what we are to the world around us and our dependence upon God. Religious truth is sorely needed if we are to avoid having a false conscience. It gives a basis for our convictions and insures their reasonableness.

In other words, conscience needs a rational support and background, and the trouble is that so many appeal to it because of sentiment and emotional reactions alone. To so act is easy because we feel commanded, we take the imperative as compelling us without realizing that the nature of the command is partly due to our built-in racial prejudices, our environment and education. Feeling here takes precedence over reasoning. Conscience has always been very plastic and at times has provided a gruesome page to history. So many crimes have been committed in its name. Leaving aside crimes, we know also how it can lead to the over-stressing of minor faults, making capital sins out of them, turning Sunday into a day of puritanical dullness, forbidding harmless joys and making God out to be a tyrant.

There is the old saying that conscience can make cowards of us! Rather should we say that if our conscience be uninformed, we lose our own integrity and fail to speak truly, sincerely or humanly. We take for granted that our conscience is afire with truth whereas it can be like a feeble light in a dark cave. Even the sophisticated are far too easily inclined to attribute only genuine or pure motivations to their own work or that of their party or trade union. Psychologists teach us a different lesson and even the greatest of saints are humble about the purity of their motives and warn aspirants of the peril of self-deceit in the pursuit of perfection.

Earlier societies were more distrustful of the claims of conscience and less sensitive to the rights of free individuals. Hence, at times, they gave short shrift to these claims if they opposed the laws of the country or of religion or ran counter to its judgments by the wise. Prudence can be pronounced by Aristotle to be the chief of the cardinal virtues and this view prevailed for many centuries. This led to harsh judgments on those guilty of what was thought to be an erroneous conscience. Here they no doubt erred in many cases; but they did not err in treating conscience as a kind of judgment in the practical order which should be well informed. Where the cases were difficult and complicated, they said one should be mod-

124

est enough to distrust one's own judgment and seek the advice of the wise and expert.

Sensible people do still seek advice, but seldom now is this recognized as a moral duty or even as a general principle to be accepted. The stress now is on the liberty of the subject and the right to judge for oneself. Conscience, as a result, has come to be regarded as an ultimate court of appeal and a safeguard of human liberties.

What then remains to be said on the subject? Obviously, each person should cultivate a sense of responsibility and impress on himself his need of an informed conscience. Thus, in his own regard and to his neighbor he should so behave as wherever possible to respect the other's liberty in choosing and assume his honesty. It is only when a person turns into a public nuisance that his liberty should be curtailed. Better to accept as a working principle patience with one's neighbor and the belief that his conscience is righteous and even nearly infallible than to treat him as a humbug and a criminal. All the same, conscience can be a treacherous companion unless we dwell in a wise milieu and with a true religion.

# XXXV

# The Messianic Hope

In the Christian tradition, the Old Testamenl and the New are joined together inseparably in one book, the Bible. Though Catholics have been accused of ignoring the Old Testament, that accusation has now much less force. They rightly disliked the habit of taking it to be so complete in itself that the actions of men and women in it could be accepted as exemplary, perfect models for Christians to follow. Today there is a clearer realization that the New Testament needs the Old for its proper understanding, and that the two have a miraculous coincidence. It is as if a great artist were to discover that his previous work had been a springboard for his final and original masterpieces. The Bible covers 1500 years and has many authors, but their writings suggest that there must have been still another author ever present, who through time worked up the material for its climax in the Gospels.

This striking impression of a drama and design developing in history can be supported and even strengthened by modern discoveries and scholarship. In contrast with other civilizations and their religions the Bible begins with a promise, and the whole history of Israel is based upon the expectation of a fulfillment of this promise. Other races look back — back to a Golden Age, and time displayed a decline from it, or if not a decline, then a constant recurrence of what must be, imaged in a wheel of fate. St. Paul wrote with justice of the Roman and Hellenic world as without hope. Hope is the keynote of Jewish history, and the Christian in turn delights in showing how Christ was the promised one, the answer to Israel's expectations.

The enthusiastic Christian is no doubt prone to exaggerate and to find parallels and analogies and anticipations which may please the heart and the aesthetic sense, but not the sober historian. Nevertheless, what struck the Jewish Apostles and evangelists was the way their past history pointed to Christ as the true Messiah, the Anointed One, the savior of Israel. St. Matthew begins his Gospel with the words, "Jesus Christ, the son of David, the son of Abraham," and continually quotes texts of the Bible as relating most properly to Christ. Our Lord himself in the beginning of his ministry chooses to read in a synagogue the words from Isaias: "The spirit of the Lord Yahweh is upon me, because Yahweh has anointed me. He has sent me to bear good tidings to the afflicted, to encourage the broken-hearted. Then, closing his talk, he declared, "Today this scripture has been fulfilled in your hearing." He identified himself with David's Lord and said that Abraham had seen his day and rejoiced. In the Transfiguration, he is attended by Elias, the supposed precursor of the Messiah, and by Moses, the law-giver of Israel who prepares it for its great destiny. At his trial he accepts the accusation of the high priest that he is the Son of God. No wonder then that St. Peter in his first sermon at Pentecost, when announcing the mission of Christ, quotes Joel's prophecy that the spirit of Yahweh was now poured forth on all esh, and later told the people of Jerusalem that Christ was the just and holy one predicted by the prophets, who would restore and renew all things. Tertullian, therefore, was not exaggerating when he exclaimed: "O Christ, old are you in your newness!"

What then was the Messianic hope which Christ fulfilled? In the Qumram Scrolls a distinction can be detected between a royal and a priestly Messiah. The sect to whom these scrolls belonged emphasized the priestly characteristic, probably owing to their hostility to the royal claims of the Hasmodeans — the Maccabean stock. As well as the priestly and royal roles, scholars assign a third, that is, a prophetic one to be played by the Messiah. In the early history of Israel, it was not until Moses had led his people to the promised land and given them the law that prophets come upon the scene. The prophet was then received — as a man sent from God to speak in God's name and to keep religion pure and undefiled among polytheist races. The prophet does not so much predict as make known God's will. So important does his figure become as God's representative that the thought of a future leader was identified with the prophet. Later, however, after kings had succeeded prophets, the ideal was held to be prefigured in the person of the royal David and to belong to his house. The Savior of the people must be of the royal line of David, himself a king. Kings, however, so often fell into idolatry and went whoring, that the law became the people's safeguard, and so the priestly line which looked after the Ark of the Covenant and the Temple regained its prestige. This importance attached to the law explains the gradual rise in authority of the scribes and Pharisees. Prophets were no longer forthcoming. Moreover, the collapse of Israel and its long exile changed its mood. A great longing for national liberation developed. Later the revolt of the Maccabees provided heroes as well as hope, heroes from whom the great deliverer might well come. Further national misfortunes served to make the heroic leader type the kind of Messiah that was favored. Hence, in the period leading up to the advent of Christ, there was a ferment of ideas and hopes, dreams and plans all the while the actual leaders often played politics or aimed at securing favor for themselves — the Herodians keeping in the good graces of Rome, the Zealots bent still on national glory, and the priestly families standing for the law. Here there was a welter of ideas, and the Messiah could be a king or priest or prophet, each party trying to interpret God's good will for his people in terms of national glory.

This situation helps us to understand the actions and reactions of the various persons and parties mentioned in the Gospels; also Our Lord's words and attitudes. Herod the Great was alarmed by the news of a child born to be king; Pilate was anxious to know exactly what the Jews meant in accusing Our Lord of wanting to rule over them. The disciples of John the Baptist felt that the Messiah must be a prophet; the Apostles for a long time clung to a crude idea of what the Master intended to do and be. Our Lord himself with the situation so confused was chary of using the title Messiah. He preferred that used by David, "the Son of Man" — the vision, that is, of "One like unto a son of man, who is brought before the Ancient of Days, invested with royalty and given an everlasting Kingship." He accepted, too, the title of Son of God, for that was how the demoniac addressed him and what Peter called him — "Thou are the Messiah, the son of the living God" — and at his death the centurion spontaneously cried: "Truly this was the Son of God." It is as if Our Lord were winnowing the various titles of their material and political bad grain and bringing them together in a superlative unity, which surpassed the hopes contained in any single one of them. He is a prophet, yet more than a prophet as declaring the will of his father, a king and yet more than a national king, because his kingdom was to embrace the whole earth, and a priest according to the order of Melchisedech, who, if needs be, will also be the victim foreseen by Isaiah.

Thus gradually disposing the minds of his hearers, Our Lord was able to unfold the incredible gift of God to man, one far beyond expectation. In the parable where the vine-dressers stone and kill the messengers of the owner, until the owner sends his own dear son to them, we read starkly but deliberately the tale of God's dealings with his chosen people. The tale is seen to be full of double meanings, to have hidden significance and an overall plot which is understood fully only at the end. When all has been said by historians of the navigable waters of the Palestinian coast line, the size and genius of its population, the benefits brought by migration and even exile, the cultural links with other nations, its series of incidents and sayings remains inexplicable except in the perspective of Christ. As a colored sail only shows its rich design when the wind blows and it is fully unfurled, so is it with the Bible in relation to Christ, and as it will be with all history, when the Son of Man returns at the end of time.

The Bible story is in itself a very human one. We see the almost irresistible attraction the surrounding world had for the Israelites, and their continual vacillation between the false gods and Yahweh, what Eliseus called their "limping on both feet." Then, too, its descriptions are lifelike. Eric Auerbach in his *Mimesis* has pointed out the contrast between the Jewish portraits and those of Homer. We watch the change in Jacob, the pet of his mother, cheating his father, working at first willingly for the sake of Rachel, so different from the old man torn by the thought that his favorite child had been ripped to pieces by a wild beast. Ulysses in the *Odyssey* is always the same vigorous, astute hero, whereas we behold the youthful David trusting in a sling and not in a great bow, a harp-player and an efficient ruler, and then sitting in old age and bewailing Absalom before he lays himself down to die. These are real individuals, not mere types; time touches them as it does not touch the Greek men and women. They resist God. They bring out in their stupidity all the mercies of Yahweh. God kneads them to his purposes, all the while accepting their free will. God makes a promise and then keeps it with Abraham and Moses, leading the Jews into a promised land. It looks as if God cared only for them, and the Israelites are vain enough to believe this. Yet Isaias tells them that all nations shall stream unto the mountain of Yahweh: "Yea, blessed be my people Egypt and Assyria, the work of my hands, and Israel my inheritance." His people are assured that the scepter shall not pass from Judah nor the staff from between his feet until *He* comes to whom it belongs. To Him shall the obedience of nations be given. Of this Messiah, the coming Savior, it is said: "Behold, a virgin shall conceive and bear a son and shall call his name Emmanuel (God with us). The Lordship shall be upon His shoulder and He will rule with wisdom and might and kindness and solicitude. The spirit of God shall rest upon this Prince of Peace." Micah foresaw that the ruler should be born in Bethlehem. The psalmist says that he will be king and priest. But alongside these promises of triumph there also came notes of sadness. He who is to come — the servant of God — will be the scorn of men, despised by his people, even though he remains one before whom all the families of the nations shall bow down. He will cry out: "My God, my God, why hast thou forsaken me?" Most striking of all in this regard is the prophecy of Isaias: "There is no beauty in him or comeliness; he is a man of sorrow and acquainted with grief . . . but if he shall lay down his life for sin, he shall have a long-lived seed."

Here then is a most extraordinary record: the history of vital men and women who are made so alive for us in their passions, loves, griefs, their savagery, their tenderness — men and women so essentially of their time and place, bargaining, lusting and quarreling; intensely individual whether we like them or dislike them; and all the while they are revealing the face of the Son of Man, rehearsing his gestures, anticipating in type what is a long way off in time, putting on Christ as like as not and in a very uncouth dress at times. They act their own self-willed parts and therewith play a part in a story which culminates in an historic drama — the life and death of Jesus Christ. Not only are the prophets engaged in unrolling future possibilities, but there is at times an astonishingly close parallel between the enacted events of the Old Testament and those of the new covenant of Christ. Witness the theme of Redemption in Abraham's assent to sacrificing his son; the abandonment of Joseph by his brothers. The exodus of the Jews may not be more than a chance symbol of the liberation of man from the servitude of sin. But the sign of blood on the doorstep which saves the first-born of the Israelites was seen by them as the guarantee of God for our salvation and was yearly celebrated in the Passover, which in turn forecasts the Last Supper and the Precious Blood quickly to flow for the world's redemption. Again the interplay of type and reality in the manna of the desert and the Bread of Life is unmistakeable. Such types accumulate, of which perhaps the most touching is David sitting between the gates hearing the news of victory, concerned alone for the safety of his evil, treacherous son Absalom. Like David, Christ wept over Jerusalem, which he would have gathered as the hen gathers its chicks, and we are the Absaloms for whom Christ cries in the words of David: "My son Absalom, Absalom my son, would to God that I might die for thee, Absalom my son."

What in isolation might seem accidental, becomes massive evidence in cumulation,

and shows that the similarities of the Old
and New Testaments are the design of God.
Like Mary, Israel bears Christ in its womb.
Christ is not only Son of Man but the Word
made Flesh. This again is a reverberation of
past sacred history, as the Ark of the Covenant and the Temple all too clearly witness. The Israelites in their wanderings carried with them the Ark in which they believed God was present in a privileged and
special manner between the two figures of
the Cherubim who crowned it. This presence
was known as the Shekinah, the Glory. In
Solomon's Temple the Shekinah or Glory
dwelt until its destruction in 586 B.C. Ezek-
iel in his eleventh chapter mourned the de-
parture of this presence from Temple and
city: "And the Glory of Yahweh rose above
the center of the city and paused upon the
hill that lies to the East," Mount Olivet.
Even in exile in Babylon the Jews hoped and
prayed for the return of the Shekinah, for
"every valley shall be filled, and the Glory
of Yahweh shall be revealed, and all flesh
shall see it." In line with the prophecies, the
fourth Gospel begins by saying that "the
Word was made Flesh and pitched His tent
among us, and we saw His Glory." With
what deliberate design these words were

138

chosen becomes still clearer when we remember that the Ark was originally a kind of
tent and that the word for "pitching the
tent" in the Greek text is almost a pun upon
the word Shekinah. Here is the Presence of
God Himself, for the words that follow call
His presence the "Glory."

The Messianic hope is completed in this
Glory. God is present, He is with us, in hu-
man shape, and He has so loved man that
He is prepared to endure the agony of the
Cross, to be as a lamb led to the slaughter
for our sake. He institutes the New Covenant
in which those who accept him will live by
his life and inherit his ancient promises.
They are to form the New Jerusalem and be
the Temple of the Holy Spirit. "Behold the
Tabernacle of God with man . . . The Lord
God is the temple thereof and the lamb."
St. John in his grand vision says: "I John
saw that holy city which is the new Jerusalem being sent down by God from heaven,
all clothed in readiness like a bride adorned
to meet her husband. And I heard a voice
which cried aloud from the throne: here is
God's tabernacle pitched among men; he
will dwell with them and be his people and
he will be among them their God. He will
wipe away every tear from their eyes and

there will be no more death or mourning, for these things have passed away."

To the Christian, the Messiah has already come. He has conquered sin and given his life lovingly as a priest for his people and he has made us into a Church which is "a chosen race, a royal pristhood, a consecrated nation." We live by faith in that glory which is the Word made Flesh, confident in his grace that our faith will one day turn into sight and reach its finale in a union with Christ closer than that of marriage — "one flesh and one spirit."

*"I Jesus, have sent my angel to give you the assurance of this; I, the root, I, the offspring of David's race, I, the bright star that brings in the day."*